D1450452

32 DAYS
ON THE
CAMINO DE
SANTIAGO

THE TRAVELOGUE OF A TOTAL AMATEUR

ALICE L. KRANZ

This book is dedicated to my girls, Haley and Izzy, to my baby grand daughter, Basil, and to my angel grand son, Baby Sage. You inspired me every day and on every step of this Camino.

Contents

Map of Camino de Santiago

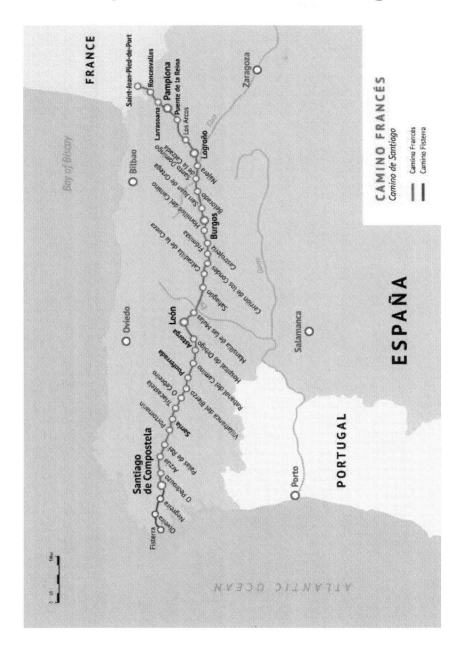

Introduction

If you're thinking about walking the Camino de Santiago, you are a pilgrim. If you're wondering how you'll find the time or the money or the information you need to walk the Camino de Santiago, you are a pilgrim. If you know in your heart that someday you'll walk the Camino de Santiago, you are a pilgrim. Your journey has already begun.

In case you were wondering...I did this by myself and you can, too. WARNING! I am not a hiker and when I began my preparation for this pilgrimage, I had ZERO experience with hiking. There was no amount of information that was too much for me to consume. I read books, watched hours of YouTube videos, joined online communities, and asked questions of anyone who would listen.

Some people might take two weeks to plan. Others might need a decade. For me, it was two years of planning and organizing. I met people who quit jobs, sold houses, gave up relationships, dropped out of college, sold everything, saved vacation days for years, retired early, delayed starting jobs, postponed weddings, and sacrificed life experience to complete this pilgrimage. When it calls you, there is no denying the force pulling you to this ancient trail.

This book is my attempt to share my experience. Use it to help plan your Camino or live vicariously through my experiences. Be inspired.

Once you walk the Camino de Santiago you will remain a pilgrim for life. It will never leave your imagination.

What is the Camino de Santiago?

The Camino de Santiago (The Way of St. James) is an ancient pilgrimage trail that leads pilgrims to the city of Santiago, where the bones of the apostle Saint James were (allegedly) buried in 44 AD. In the middle ages (around 1100 to 1450 AD), people believed that pilgrims who walked this trail and received a certificate of pilgrimage would spend less time in purgatory. During this era, the Knights Templar played a role in protecting pilgrims on this trail. The effects of this organization are still present in the 21st century. Over its hundreds of years of existence, an entire economy has emerged around the Camino, with villages, cities, churches, cathedrals, and services all specifically to support pilgrims.

Some of the more popular pilgrimage routes include:
- Camino Francis
- Camino Portuguese
- Camino Norte
- Camino Primitivo
- Camino Madrid

Where will you begin your Camino?

Remember, if you are even THINKING about attempting the Camino de Santiago, you have already begun your Camino.

End of Day 5 on the Camino de Santiago.

How did I get there?

Greensburg, Pennsylvania to NYC Penn Station (Amtrak train)

Penn Station to JFK (subway)

JFK to Paris (plane)

Paris to Lyon, France (high speed train) (spent a few days with friends)

Lyon, France to train station (taxi)

Lyon train station to airport (train)

Leaving from the train station in Greensburg, Pennsylvania.

Lyon, France to Biarritz, France (plane)

Biarritz airport to Bayonne, France hotel (taxi)

Bayonne hotel to train station (walked across the street)

Bayonne train station to St. Jean Pied de Port (train)

St. Jean Pied de Port to Santiago (walked)

Santiago to London (plane) (spent a week with friends)

London to Scotland (plane) (spent a week with friends)

Scotland to Pittsburgh (plane)

Pittsburgh to Greensburg (car)

What gear did I use?

- Backpack (45L)
- Rain cover for backpack
- Walking poles (purchased in SJPP)
- Small fanny pack
- iPhone
- European charger specifically for my iPhone
- Headphones
- 2 small wallets for two different currencies
- Cash: $100 US dollars and €100 Euros
- 1 ATM card
- 1 credit card
- Passport
- Driver's license
- Medical insurance card
- 2 packing cubes (one for clothes and one for everything else)
- Small pocket knife
- Hat
- Headlamp
- Sunglasses
- Sunscreen and lip balm with sunscreen
- Rain jacket and rain pants
- Sleep sack

I started with this backpack, but I ended with a different one.

- Microfiber towels (1 medium size and 1 extra small size)
- Another microfiber towel, purchased on the Camino (see *Day 6: New Microfiber Towel*)
- 2 pairs of shorts
- 1 pair of leggings
- 3 shirts/1 tank top
- 1 yoga dress
- 3 pairs of undergarments
- 1 REI long sleeve quarter zip shirt that's not a fleece but kind of like one only thinner but super warm
- 2 pairs of Smartwool socks (I didn't wear them because they gave me a rash around my ankles that I call the ring of fire.)
- 2 pairs of trekking socks, purchased on the Camino (The only ones I wear.)
- 1 pair of sock liners
- Adidas® trail shoes (I hate them with a passion.)
- Chaco® trail sandals
- Flip flops, purchased on the Camino
- Lush bar shampoo/spray conditioner/small hairbrush
- Deodorant
- Toothbrush & toothpaste, floss
- Q-tips®/tweezers/razor
- Contact lens case & solution/extra contacts
- Glasses & glasses case
- ZzzQuil® sleep aid
- Several zip lock baggies
- Small journal with pen/black sharpie
- Camino Guidebook by John Brierley

Alice's Camino Glossary

There are some words, phrases, idioms, and Camino lingo that you might not have heard before. Most of these were COMPLETELY NEW to me. I learned them along the way.

Albergue: A place to sleep. Albergues are similar to hostels, but they are specifically for pilgrims. You must present your **pilgrim's passport** to get a bed. They may have anywhere from ten to 200 beds. They may also have showers, clothes washing facilities, kitchens, indoor and outdoor spaces, restaurants, convenience stores, backpack transfer services, religious services, or medical services like massages and foot care provided by medical students. You might sleep in a bunk next to a total stranger. Yes, you might be using the same bathroom as the opposite sex. We all grew up with brothers and sisters so don't make a big deal out of it. If it's a huge problem for you, consider staying in a private hotel or private albergue with a private room. (Boring!) The first time you stand in a bathroom and brush your teeth next to a total stranger of the opposite sex, remember it. It's a unique Camino experience.

Alto: A climb, a summit.

Buen Camino: A greeting between pilgrims and locals along the trail. Spanish for "good road" or "good path", literal or metaphorical.

Café con leche: The best coffee with milk that you will ever drink in your entire life. Period.

Camino Candy: See also: **milagro** and **sixies**. Anything that takes away the pain and helps you make it through the day. Available from **farmicias** found along the Camino. I always spoke with the pharmacist in charge before I took any medications. I'M NOT TELLING YOU TO TAKE DRUGS! But if you need pain relief, it is available.

Compeed®: Hydrocolloid gel cushions that stick to your feet. See also: **Second skin/mole skin/liquid skin.**

Compression socks: Extremely tight-fitting socks that are supposed to alleviate swelling of your feet and/or legs. Some people swear by them.

Credencial del Peregrino: See also: **credential** and **pilgrim's passport**. On this document you will record your journey with a series of stamps that you acquire along the way. You will pick up this document at a **pilgrim's office** when you begin your Camino (they usually cost €2-3) and show it as proof of your pilgrimage in Santiago. Stamps are a source of pride for pilgrims. Each one is unique and clever. Take time to appreciate the uniqueness of each stamp. You will get stamps in albergues, cafes, bars, stores, shops, churches, roadside stands, etc. You must acquire two stamps per day for the last 100k of the Camino in order to get your official Pilgrims credential in Santiago.

Credential: See also **Credencial del Peregrino** and **pilgrim's passport**.

Donatovio: Spanish for donation. As you make your way along the Camino, you will find that you don't need as much stuff as you think. To be honest, you need about 25% less than what is on your current packing list. You will get rid of at least 15% more of that "stuff" within the first two days. Most albergues have a place to donate your stuff. Get rid of it. Remember that the weight of your pack is directly proportionate to the size of your fears. That heavy pack means you are SCARED TO DEATH. Understandable. You'll gain confidence as you walk and you won't be afraid any more. You will start to unburden yourself from all the stuff you don't need. Read that last line again. Yes, it is a metaphor.

Farmacia: Spanish for pharmacy.

Milagro: Spanish for MIRACLE. This is a word we used for an anti-pain/anti-inflammatory medicine we learned about on the Camino. The Spanish name for the product I took was called "enantyum" and it is a clear liquid that comes in a tube. In the United States, you would need a prescription for this, but most medicine in Spain does not require a prescription. Obviously, consult with your doctor and ask the pharmacist before you take anything like this, especially if you are taking any other medications. For me, this was a life saver. I don't know that I could have made it through the Camino without hardcore pain meds. I took this only a handful of times. WORTH IT!

Municipal: These albergues are usually run by volunteers and host large numbers of pilgrims. They are the most affordable and often the most crowded. Some are basic and some have many services. Most have beds with linens (often plastic), pillows and blankets. Keep in mind that hundreds of pilgrims pass through these facilities every day and they get tons of wear and tear during the high season. If you're expecting even one star accommodations don't stay here because you will be disappointed. Every albergue is different so you will see some are better cared for than others. What do you expect for five, six or seven euros a night?

Nara: A brand of orange soda found along the Camino. (My fave.)

Perfectly normal: Things that you see along the Camino that outside of that space would seem bizarre, but on the Camino it's perfectly normal. For example, pilgrims sitting on the side of the Camino **wicking** each other's blisters while at the same time eating chocolate.

Pilgrim's office: This is a location for pilgrims to check in, obtain a pilgrim's passport, pick up information on albergues, weigh your backpack, buy a pilgrim's shell, and meet people who will walking the Camino at the same time as you. Pilgrim's offices are open year around but have set hours. They are only located in major cities and starting points for the Camino. A little fun fact is that these offices often have free Wi-Fi, and even if the office is closed, you can still pick up a signal if you are hoovering close by.

Pilgrim's passport: See also: **Credencial del Peregrino** and **credential**.

Potable and non-potable water: Potable water is you CAN drink, and non-potable is water you CANNOT drink. Use a water bladder like a CamelBak that fits in your pack so you can drink water while you walk. Get the kind with a spout that opens and closes. Remember to CLOSE it after you take a drink or your water will drip out, and you won't know until it's too late. Your water will stay surprisingly cold during the day and you'll thank yourself a million times for having it so accessible. I filled mine every night before bed because it was one less thing to do before leaving in the morning. There is plenty of water on the Camino, but it's one less thing for you to worry about.

Second Breakfast: After walking for 2-3 hours first thing in the morning you're going to want to eat a full breakfast again. It's not difficult to understand why!

Second skin/mole skin/liquid skin: Blister treatment techniques that did not work for me, but others have had some level of success with these pre-walking treatments; just wear bigger shoes and let the blisters form a callus that will eventually go numb. See also: **Compeed®**.

Sixies: Ibuprofen 600 that you can buy over the counter at the **farmacia**. They are stronger than the ibuprofen that's typically available in the United States. Consult your doctor!

Stamps: Unique stamps you will acquire for your **pilgrim's passport** along the Camino

Threading: Treating blisters using a sewing needle with thread. Push the needle through the blister and pull the thread through the skin so that the thread allows the fluid to drain. Cut the tread from the needle with about an inch or two of thread hanging out from both sides of the blister. It's **perfectly normal** to thread a blister and continue walking. (See also: **wicking**.)

Tortilla: A breakfast/**second breakfast**/lunch food. It is essentially a type of quiche, with various ingredients such as meat, potatoes, and/or vegetable. This can be eaten alone or on a crusty bread. Delicious and filling.

Waymarkers:
Yellow arrows
painted at
predictable and
sometimes
unpredictable
places along the
Camino.
Waymarkers are
sometimes a
yellow shell set
against a blue
background. Your
heart will beat
through your
chest if you walk

A waymarker on the Camino de Santiago.

too long without seeing one, but at that exact moment
you'll see it and everything in the world will be right
again. For the rest of your life, you will never again
look at a yellow arrow and not think of the Camino.

Wicking: Treating blisters using a sewing needle with
thread. (See also: **threading**.)

Zig Zag: When attempting to walk an extremely steep
mountain you might walk in a zig zag pattern to take
some of the weight off your body. Also, when
attempting a steep downhill climb walking in a zig zag
pattern might help to prevent blisters or extreme
muscle strain. Also called switchbacks.

Pre-Camino

Bayonne, France

After spending time with friends in Lyon, I took a plane to Biarritz, then a taxi to Bayonne where I had booked a hotel directly across the street from the train station. For most of that day I walked around the city, bought some food, and began my transformation from civilian to pilgrim.

In the morning I got on the train to the small village of St. Jean Pied de Port. The train ride took about an hour, and on that train I met some of the pilgrims who were with me the entire way to Santiago.

In front of the Bayonne train station. 75% Pilgrim Transformation.

St. Jean Pied de Port, France

It's HOT in France today. I'm already swampy and
sweaty to the core, and I don't even start the hard
work until tomorrow. Tomorrow I will walk over the
Pyrenees Mountains and cross the border into Spain.
It's 18 miles uphill and I'm so pumped and ready that I
want to start NOW. But I must first have a communal
dinner with the members of my albergue, TRY to sleep,
and wait until 6:15 am to meet up with some
Americans I met on the train. Then begin.

St. Jean Pied de Port.

*100% Pilgrim
Transformation.*

See those mountains in the distance? Yup, that's what happening tomorrow.

The Pyrenees from the village of St. Jean Pied de Port.

Day 1: Today was HORRIBLE

St. Jean Pied de Port (SJPP) to Roncesvalles
18 miles over the mountain in the heat
6:15am to 4:30pm

Let's get this out of way. Today was HORRIBLE. Probably the most physically challenging thing I've ever done. I have so many problems right now:

- Blisters
- Probably going to lose some toenails
- My shoulders/back/hips—all in pain
- Sunburned
- Slightly heat sick, probably mild dehydration

Rest stop. No shade.

Yes! I promise I did everything to prepare for this day and in reality there is no way to prepare.

At times it was so steep I felt like Michael Jackson in the Smooth Criminal video. Like the steepest staircase you can imagine, and it goes on for miles and miles and I'm carrying 16-17 pounds on my back and it's 97 degrees and virtually no shade. It was more awful than I can describe.

At the summit, the air is so thin and every time I try to take a breath all I get is the smell of cow/horse/sheep crap. I can taste it. I drank so much water and I PEED ONE TIME ALL DAY!! I drank at least three liters of water. Applied sunscreen, three times, stopped frequently for breaks, stood in the shade when I could find it, took off my pack and rested, trudged on SLOWLY.

First day on the Camino with my friend, Alex.

The worst part is the downhill.

I have a little Camino family. Alex, who started in Paris, walked for seven days, couldn't take the heat, jumped on a train to SJPP and now she's my Camino Mom. She's only 28. Jim, who we met on the train over. We could not have made it today without each other. We didn't really talk much because we were so focused on surviving. Occasionally we'd burst into rounds of cursing everything and hating life. We made an excellent trifecta.

I have no idea how I'm going to get through tomorrow.

Middle of the night
Roncesvalles Albergue in the Pyrenees Mountains

It's 4:00 am and I've been up since 3:30 am STARVING, so I got up to eat something and the Wi-Fi is STRONG.

There are so many people here from all over the world.
- France
- Spain
- Sweden
- Italy
- Australia
- Germany
- Switzerland
- United States
- Korea

TONS of Koreans. Like noticeably a lot. My favorite (you guys know I have my favorites!) is a kid who I met outside the pilgrim's office two days ago. Such a big smile and perfect hair. I started talking to him and OMG his English is perfect. I asked him if he likes K-Pop and he was so excited I knew about K-Pop. Korean pop music: do yourself a favor and watch some videos today. So entertaining. I call him Gangnam Style and he LOVES IT. He told me to call him Psy for short.

View from the top of the Pyrenees.

Yesterday we met a Korean walking in the OPPOSITE direction. He only had a short amount of time and couldn't do the whole

Camino so he only walked here to Roncesvalles to overnight then back to SJPP. He was so sweet! I think it's interesting how they call themselves Korean and everyone is quick to ask, "South Korean?" I've heard this many times. I love that they are just Korean. Period. They don't separate themselves into north and south.

I can sleep so much better because it's cool up here in the mountains. Also, there are not so many bugs and flies in the room like in SJPP. One of my fears is that a bug is going to fly into my mouth while I'm sleeping, because I know for a fact that I sleep like a dead person with my mouth open.

One more thing... I was aware of this already, but Steeler Nation is strong around the world. Everyone around the world knows this team. When I say I'm from Pittsburgh, they all congratulate me on the Penguins winning the Stanley Cup.

Finally arrived at the albergue.

Day 2: Couldn't See the Hemingway Piano

Roncesvalles to Zuribi
13.6 miles (8 hours)
Miles to go: 453.1

Today started out to be 1000 times better than yesterday.

We began at 6:00 am and this amazing thing was happening...it was slightly chilly outside. And the first part of the day was flat and fast.

We came to the town of Burgette, which is a significant location in Hemingway's *The Sun Also Rises*. The village remains largely unchanged since that time. Since the 18th century, to be more exact. We passed

The church next to my albergue in Roncesvalles.

through several of these villages and farms that remain frozen in time. There is a piano in a hostel here which is signed by Hemingway, but when we tried to look we got a hard NO. It's still a working hostel and I think pilgrims are an annoyance.

This is my life as a pilgrim:
- Get up early and walk all day until I arrive at a destination, usually chosen the night before
- Arrive in the village where I want to stay
- Look for accommodations
- Take a shower
- Wash my clothes in the sink
- Hang them to dry
- Try to figure out the Wi-Fi situation
- Go around the village to look for food/provisions (Note: siesta until 5:30 pm in Spain!)
- Eat
- Update Facebook—these daily stories eventually will become this book! Organize my pack for the next day
- Sleep
- Repeat

Open air surgery, "wicking" my blisters. You basically thread some string through a blister and just leave it. It went numb after about 30-40 minutes of walking. I walked about 12 miles on this today.

Really steep uphill. With rocks. For about four miles. Only about 85 degrees today.

My new German friend, Gim (pronounced Yim) had to be taken by ambulance last night and given two bags of IV fluid after the walk yesterday. He was driven back to the hostel and he's back at it today. He's 20 and just finished school and immediately left to do the Camino. Alone. A German father and son randomly met him this morning and walked the whole day with him to keep him healthy. The Camino provides you with a family at the exact moment you need one. He's 6'7". He learned how to speak perfect English from watching YouTube videos.

Gim on the Camino.

Day 3: Nutella

Zubiri to Pamplona
14 miles / 9 hours

Everyone walks his or her own Camino. Yeah, we create our little Camino family and spend the hours and days walking together, but in reality, we are alone. These paths and trails are not easy. Hills, trails, steep, rocky, heat, heavy, exhaustion. There is not as much idle conversation as you'd imagine. We all walk for

The waymarker I've been looking for!

deeply personal reasons that can't be explained. Our packs are heavy. They're a burden, just like the things we carry in our lives. As we move along this trail we slowly start to remove things from our packs to lighten the load. Is it worth it to carry that extra weight? Do I need it, or can I survive without it? Packs get lighter, things get eliminated, fears start to disappear.

We follow the waymarkers, that are symbolized by the yellow shell or just a yellow arrow. The path is clearly marked, but there are times I walk for an hour or more and see no signs. Panic creeps in. Wait, was I supposed to turn there? Did I miss the trail? Why haven't I seen anything? OMG, what if I have to walk back? My body can't take anymore walking! And then boom, a yellow arrow exactly at the moment I need it.

2nd Breakfast.

What I ate today:
1st breakfast: protein bar & apple
2nd breakfast: cheese & tomato baguette, banana, orange soda, & three ibuprofen
Snack 1: cherries, crackers with Nutella
Yes, I'm carrying a small jar of Nutella in my pack. Zero regrets.
Snack 2: 1/2 bag of nuts
Dinner tonight: TBD, but probably tapas. Because SPAIN.

I'm staying at the municipal hostel in PAMPLONA tonight. It costs €8 a night and it's got over 100 beds for pilgrims only. The bathroom is co-ed so we all use the toilet and shower in the same place. It takes less than 30 seconds to get over it.

I'm dying to explore the city, but I cannot move at moment.

Things I wish I had:
- More ibuprofen
- Flip flops
- A side zip pack

- Better trail shoes that are a whole size bigger than I usually wear, not just a half size bigger
- Better sunscreen

All smiles, because I put on my sandals.

My bed in Pamplona.

Day 4: Italian Eating Rituals

Pamplona to Puente la Reina
16+ miles (a long walk today)

It is 63 degrees at 5:30 am this morning in Pamplona,
Spain. Last night I saw the hotel balcony from where
Hemingway viewed the running of the bulls, but all I
can think about is the blister on my pinky toe.

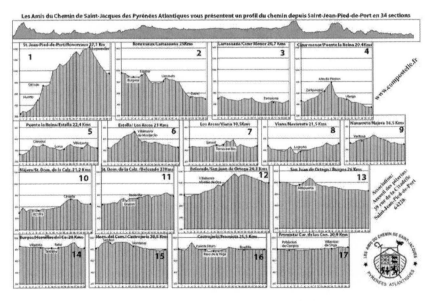

Elevation changes on seventeen stages of the Camino.
*(Image from **A Pilgrims Guide to The Camino de**
Santiago by John Brierley.)*

This is an altitude chart of the first half of the Camino. Today is day four. It looks manageable on paper, but in reality, that little peak is going to be extremely challenging. (Understatement!)

All we want is a flat trail, but life isn't like that, is it?

I'm hoping to arrive in Santiago on July 25.

There is a legend on the trail that a pilgrim was walking the Camino and ran out of water. The devil appeared and told him, "I will give you water, but you must first give up your faith." The pilgrim said no, and continued walking. Very soon after, St. James came to thank him and brought with him a seashell full of water. That is one reason why pilgrims always carry a seashell.

There is an American family (grandma, mother, and 13-year-old daughter) who met a Spanish family (father, 15-year-old son, and 13-year-old daughter). These two families now walk every day together, and the Spanish brother translates for the two 13-year-old best friends. Sometimes I walk with them, too.

Yesterday and today I walked mostly with the Italians. Marta, Sara, Selana, Antonio, Marco, Fabrizo, and

Mikele, who turned 22 years old today. My Camino Mom Alex, the Brit called Stewart, another American named Josh, and Pablo the Argentinian were always close by.

My early Camino family. (That's me, second from the right.)

When you walk with Italians, you get to

listen to them talk. I never get tired of listening to their chatter. They also speak English, and they tell me stories about Southern Italy vs. Northern Italy. Laid back, easy going, no worries, vs. busy, work too much, stressed out.

When you walk with Italians, be prepared for the eating rituals. There is never a time when you just grab something to eat and quickly move on.

Every eating situation is an event. There is laughter, eating, relaxing, and ALWAYS sharing the food. If an Italian opens a bottle, a package of food, a bag of something, you will always be offered the first bite, taste, drink. If food is ordered, you will be served first, always. Sara was treating her blisters today, and in the middle she offered me some chocolate she had in her bag. Marta also had chocolate which got passed around.

It's fun to go shopping with three Italians who are preparing a communal meal for 15 people. So much discussion about the tomatoes.

Grocery Shopping with Italians. Puente La Renia, Spain.

It is impossible to not mention the feet situation. It's bad. My poles were used more like crutches today. The blisters usually go numb, but not today. Only when I switched to my sandals did the pain go from 100% to 70%. A massive improvement. The path was hard today, as it is every day. My body is getting stronger and my stamina is excellent, but my feet! Why can't I just have my feet! That's the main thing I need to walk! There are 29 days to go.

Things I don't do anymore:
- Wear make-up
- Brush my hair

Things I do now:
- Wash my clothes in the shower while I'm taking a shower
- Fill up my CamelBak in a sink that says "you may wash your shoes in this sink"
- Wear a buff
- Wear socks with sandals
- Have an adult conversation while picking my feet and/or watching feet get picked

Medic Mike, who taught me how to take care of my feet.

Blister wicking with Sara from Italy.

Perfectly normal to see feet like this.

Sometimes we walk in a group of eight, or five, or three, or solo, or six again. Sometimes I don't see another pilgrim for more than an hour. But I always see the waymarkers.

Walking across ancient trails.

Approaching a village café and seeing pilgrims at rest.

Dos huevos for breakfast.

Alton de Perdon. (Yes, I took this pic.)

Famous monument dedicated to the pilgrims at the peak.

Day 5: Three Pieces of Ice

Puente La Reina to Estella
Attempting stage 5 of the Camino Frances, which is
only 13.5 miles.

I remember telling people before I did this that it is a walk across Spain. WRONG! This is a hike! For advanced hikers and outdoors people! Prior to this I had never done a real hike in my life.

Good news: Woke up with feet at 65% capacity.

6:00 am leaving Puente La Renia.

(Yesterday we were at less than 20%.)

Bad news: Projected rain and thunderstorms.

We always start out with eight or 12 but end up spreading out over the day, often walking alone but together.

This morning, Mikele was waiting with our group to begin. I asked him about the tattoo on his leg. It says "my life is brilliant" with a little star. He said he loves the song by James Blunt, and the star represents his mom who he loves more than anything in life. He was tearing up. He said he was so worried about spending his birthday alone on the Camino. Now he has so many friends, but he misses his mama so much. I love the Italians!

Downhill is THE WORST.

It was one hour and thirty-five minutes before anyone spoke. We walked in silence this morning, three of us girls. We are all suffering greatly from blisters, aches, pains, burdens, the heavy packs, fear of rain, the unfamiliar terrain. How many hills? Can we do this? So much uncertainty, we couldn't even speak to each other. All in our heads with our thoughts and fears. I detest a morning talker, so it was perfect. We stopped at a bar after almost two hours. I ate some nuts and bought a small bottle of pineapple juice for two euro.

So much time is spent looking down during the day. One wrong step, it's a sprained ankle, trip and fall on my face, any injury could be a disaster.

Steep Roman roads.

So much time is spent in the countryside, rural roads, ancient villages, old Roman buildings, signage that dates back to the 13th, 14th, 15th century.

We stopped for lunch at a cafe in one of these villages. I had a ham, cheese & tomato baguette, my favorite orange soda and a nectarine for €5.

If you are walking up a hill and really struggling to the point that you must stop and rest every few steps and pilgrims pass you at a steady pace with no effort or any detectable sweat or struggle whatsoever they are Swiss or German, guaranteed.

I saw my favorite boyfriend/girlfriend couple from Estonia playing in the river today. They are so young and speak excellent English. They stayed right next to me last night in the albergues. I noticed that they

travel with a bottle of vodka and a bottle of orange juice. The three of us shared a drink before bed.

Sara and I limped into the village today. She's only 21 and came here alone. The rest of the Italians have arrived, but I cannot move from this bed. I would pay so much money for someone to bring Sara and I dinner in bed.

Fake smile. The fact I'm wearing sandals means it's an intense-feet-pain kind of day.

Good things on the Camino:
- ice for your beverage (three ice cubes max)
- a cafe with food at the exact moment you're starving
- a bottom bunk
- showers with a hook
- seeing friends you haven't seen for a few days
- random strangers will carefully examine your blisters and even offer to "wick" them with string
- the Italians

Bad things on the Camino:
- when you drop your poles and have to bend over to pick them up while wearing your pack
- bugs that get caught up in your orbit and are hard to shoo away
- mosquito bites

The main thing I wish I could show you guys are the doors, so I took lots of pics of them today.

For the love of doors.

Estella, Spain
At the end of a long day

If you need some travel inspiration, google Estella, Spain and look at pictures.

Views of Estella, Spain. From my bed.

The Nun and Me

We alone were on a very steep, rocky hill. She in her habit and long sleeves, polyester and hot. Me in head-to-toe moisture wicking fabrics, sun protection shirt, shorts, hat. We both had walking sticks. The hill was steep so each step was carefully considered. I would walk five steps and wait for her, and then she would walk five steps and wait for me. We continued this way up the steep hill, both of us panting and sweaty. Her

Walking with my Camino sister, the nun.

internal journey is holy and thankful for every step. My internal journey is cursing all of creation and why the hell did I think this was a good idea?

Whose idea was it to put boulders on a cliff where pilgrims are walking?!

The view from our peak. (Picture courtesy of my iPhone.)

I made it to the top first and waited for her. My legs were shaking like jelly. We both turned around to look at the view. She looked with her eyes and I took a photo with my iPhone. I finally looked at her for the first time and she looked at me and nodded. We never spoke. My Camino sister.

Day 6: New Microfiber Towel

Estella to Los Acros
A little over 18 miles today

Drank wine from a monastic font today

When I woke up this morning, I felt well rested. Right now it is 66 degrees and raining. Wet feet + blisters = I don't know yet.

Early this morning we came upon a monastic font at Monasterio de Irache. I read somewhere that this wine is supposed to provide motivation to weary pilgrims. It was tasty. Light, refreshing, sweet, nourishing.

Now? At the end of the day? Totally spent. I don't even really know where I am. Today was way too much. This whole thing is hard. I don't remember what I thought it was going to be like but it's nothing like I imagined. I am totally unprepared for this in every way. My gear is all wrong, including my pack and shoes...hate them. I have planned 33 days to walk to Santiago and so far only completed six. Hold on for one more day.

There are Roman ruins, ancient villages, farms, agricultural, animals, very little civilization at times. We always have to climb a hill to get to a village.

Today after almost two hours of nothing, no villages, no cafes, no roads, just rural farms with not a person, car or road in sight, we saw in the distance a food truck, and there were tables and shade. As we got closer, we could hear music. Right when we arrive, literally limping, shuffling, and completely exhausted, dead set on getting into the shade, Wilson Phillips "Hold On for One More Day" came on. We walked in screaming the lyrics at the top of our lungs. These young Italian girls know every word.

I used my GoGirl today. Twice. It works perfectly. (Google it.)

Good decisions I made about gear:
- My cocoon sleep sack
- Zachary Gaskell's boy scout knife. I use it every day. Thanks, Zach!
- Chaco® sandals
- Moisture wicking everything
- Walking poles
- CamelBak water bag
- My hat
- The new buff I got in Pamplona
- A small microfiber hand towel, the size of a handkerchief. I use it all day, every day.
- Two microfiber towels. On Day 2, I bought a second microfiber towel because it is impossible to dry off with wet hair. I love it! Massive improvement, but I would give it up for a pair of flip flops.

Everything else sucks.

The Wi-Fi is so weak at the albergue in Los Acros and I am too tired to go find better so this is a picture of me at the beginning of the day and end of the day.

All is good.

Day 6: Before

Day 6: After

I know there's pain.
Why do you lock yourself up in these chains?
No one can change your life except for you.
Don't you know things can change?
Things'll go your way if you hold on for one more day.
Can you hold on for one more day?
Things will go your way, hold on for one more day.

—"Hold On For One More Day" by Wilson Phillips

Camino sisters representing Italy, Spain and the United States. We all started off solo, but now we are together.

Day 7: Still Carrying the Nutella

Los Acros to Logroño
18.2 miles

Two words: Flip flops.

I got flip flops today.

It's only 10:00 am and we've already done ten km, which is halfway to today's destination. We'll arrive by 1:00 pm and have time to relax. This is a supreme luxury.

My blisters are SO MUCH BETTER! Today is the first day I walk with only 15% pain.

My second breakfast. It was raining and it got a little soggy but I crushed it anyway.

Isn't there a saying that to attain knowledge you add things every day, but to attain wisdom, remove things every day? So in that spirit, I left my Nutella in Estella. (It rhymes!) Also, I ate my apple and orange and I'm not going to carry fruit anymore because it's too heavy. There's always fruit to buy everywhere. I ditched my sock liners for today and smothered my feet in Compeed® and am right now airing feet and then changing socks.

Shopping in Logroño, Spain

Viana; (he was scraping up bird poop in front of the church).

Starting off the day with my girls Sara, Marta and of course a little rain to keep it interesting.

Right after this picture was taken it started pouring down rain.

When you are walking on the Camino de Santiago in the North of Spain and on the 8th day you want to give up and take a bus or just lay down and cry and there is no cafe in sight for hours you find a bridge, lay down your rain jacket and then wait patiently for someone to pass by and take your picture. Still 9km to go and it's already 3pm. Probably three more hours of walking.

Marta from Italy and me.

Day 8: Today I Cried HARD

Logroño to Nájera
18+ miles today

I had my first meltdown today.

When we left town, we spent a good hour walking through a Central Park type area and I thought it was going to be a good day when I saw a cocker spaniel walking alone with a toy pig in its mouth. Every time it squeaked, it made an oinking sound. Everything went awful after that.

It was slow going today. We left at 6:10am and arrived at 6pm. That's almost 12 hours of walking. Too much.

At 10:00 am I took a 600mg ibuprofen and at 2:00 pm I took a pharmacy edition of some kind of liquid pain killer (milagro) from Medic Mike and then 600mg of Motrin at 6:30 pm. I'm barely keeping it together. Feet pain is the primary issue. Body pain is the secondary issue.

At 3:00 pm we were within ten km of our destination and as soon as we began walking, the wind kicked in and blew HARD for three hours. We were walking up hill and the wind was blowing down on us. I wish I was making this up. Sara and I talked about taking a bus to our next destination to salvage our bodies for tomorrow. We even tried sending our packs using a courier service. Too late, we missed the cutoff time. The last three hours with the wind was like getting a Camino exfoliation with the dirt and sand blowing a constant stream of debris.

And there was rain today, downpours that just dump and move on. It turns the path into a muddy sludge and even though we're not walking in water the dirt and mud kicks up on the back of your legs and your butt. I wish I was making this up.

No matter how much you prepare, this much walking can be brutal. When we left at 3pm for the last 10k we were a group of nine. We broke into different groups with different strides. I could see a group of three in front of me, 200 meters ahead, then 300 meters. I was completely alone. No one in front of me and no one back of me. Not one single soul on the trail. The gap kept growing and I was thinking that's two times around the track, I can catch up. At least I could see them. And then I couldn't see them anymore. This went on for more than two hours! But I knew they were up ahead. Keep going. Ignore the pain.

Two hours went by and I was still alone on the trail. Not one single person in my sight for two hours. My feet were SHREDDED. I knew it was getting late because the temperature shifted and it began to cool down. The sun was more down than up. And I had no idea how long to the village, where is the albergue, are there going to be beds available, should I just lay down on this trail and get out of the wind, are my feet seriously bleeding, where am I? I just kept walking.

Then I saw my Camino brother Josh waiting for me at a corner that led into town and I lost it. I cried when I saw him. We walked another 45 minutes to the village, to the albergue and I really did use my sticks as crutches but I made it. Eighteen miles.

And here's the best part. When I finally got to take a shower there was only cold water. True story.

Day 9: A Camino Love Story

Nájera to Santo Domingo
Only a paltry 13 miles today
132 miles so far

The morning after my worst day on the Camino.

Left over pizza, juice, Advil, a good night's sleep, a little chill in the air and I'm feeling better this morning. Ready to take on this next 13 miles.

The Camino de Santiago is a very ancient and sacred trail that has been traveled upon for a thousand years. Pilgrims who walk on this road have gone through exactly what I'm going through right now. The way to Santiago consists of various trails. Some begin in Rome, Paris, Germany, Madrid, Le Puy, Portugal, and Greensburg, Pennsylvania. For a thousand years, pilgrims who have walked here have left a little bit of themselves on this road. Blood, sweat, tears, fear, pain, regrets, and resentments. All of this gets mixed into the dirt, rocks, grass and water and it becomes the ingredients for that Camino spirit. Yesterday I left all of that and more on the Camino.

Yesterday the Camino spirt pushed me along that trial. It was equally horrible and beautiful.

Jessica is from Spain and this is her second time on the Camino. She walked from Sarria to Santiago and earned her certification as a pilgrim, but she wanted more so

Pilgrims at rest along the Camino.

she came back to walk the full Camino Frances. She lives in a village outside of Barcelona and she is DROP DEAD GORGEOUS! When she was 17 she opened her own dance school with five students. Now, almost ten years later, her dance school teaches over 200 kids. Her last boyfriend broke up with her because he found another girl. Idiot!

Marco is a very sweet Italian boy from a small village. He's quiet, but extremely observant. His gentlemanly ways make him popular with the group, and he speaks excellent English. He sometimes gives Jessica a flower and sometimes they walk together. The chemistry is palpable. Today I walked with Jessica for a few hours and laughed the whole time because she could perfectly imitate my American accent. Tonight she leaves us and Marco will continue to Santiago.

It's cold and rainy on the Camino this morning so we have paused for second breakfast.

I am so happy today because my friend Jamie HAD HER BABY and he is so perfect.

And as if that wasn't good enough, I feel excellent today. Already halfway to today's destination, and it's a smooth trail.

2nd breakfast with my 1st Camino friend, Alex.

 Those small village roads never let me down. When I walk into a village I imagine thousands of pilgrims have walked here before and they have seen the same roads and towns and farms.

If it wasn't me doing this I would be intensely curious about so many things, like money. How much does everything cost? This is what I have spent today and it's a very typical day:

Chocolate croissant, €1.20.
Apple and some cut watermelon from a vendor on the trail...donativo so I gave him €1.
Small ice cream cone in a café, €1.
My room for the night, €7.
Dinner tonight with the Italians €2. (We shop and cook and everyone pitches in.)
Going to get a snack in a cafe soon, €3.50.
Splurged on laundry rather than doing it by hand, €5.50.

You can see, it's relatively cheap. I save money because I don't go out every night to eat. I buy groceries to eat on the road. Or I eat what Mikele cooks, which is better than any restaurant around.

The pilgrim's hostels are cheap and perfectly adequate. You must be willing to give up modesty and fully embrace communal living. It's like everything else, you get used to it.

Typical Camino Albergue.

Dinner with my Italian family.

Day 10: Here I Go Again

June 30, 2017
Santo Domingo to Belorado
14 miles
Approximately 146 miles total (who knows?)

There was a huge Italian party last night. I'll get to that in a minute.

Morning feet preparation.

It appears that 13 miles is the sweet spot for me. Don't get me wrong, there has never been a day without pain, limping, blisters, hills, dirt, rocks, rain, heat, and OMG that wind! Those last three to four miles are always the most painful. No matter what, my feet are going to hurt, I've accepted that.

Medic Mike and I stood in a poppy field today. He threads my blisters after dinner almost every night.

Morning routine is eat and feet. I can't remember what it's like to just get up and go because I'm always tending to blisters.

Today is another long day and it's FREEZING! Like 40s and 50s all day so I'm wearing all my clothes and socks on my hands.

Tomorrow is a 15-mile day and the next is a 16-mile day. I know there's another 18 day thrown in the mix somewhere. Maybe even two of them.

We had to say goodbye to four members of our family of pilgrims last night. Keep in mind, we all arrived solo and now we have formed a family. But not everyone has the time to commit 35-40 days so they will walk the Camino in sections as time permits. The hardest for me was losing Marta because she, Sara, and I have walked together for so many days. She's going to be following us on Facebook, but her absence is a major loss for us. She speaks broken English and I speak zero Italian, but we somehow formed an incredible bond. I will miss her dearly. Which brings me to our party. Mikele, the sweetest 22-year old Italian kid cooks for us EVERY SINGLE NIGHT. Last night we were a party of 20. He began dinner preparations at 4pm and we sat down to eat at 9pm. We had SO

MUCH FOOD! He said that it makes him so happy to watch everyone devour his cooking. This is a kid who carries three items in his wallet: a picture of Jesus, a picture of his sister (diagnosed as severely autistic) and a picture of his mama. This Italian kid is my whole heart!

Everyone claps when dinner is finally served. My love for the Italians is infinite.

If you are wondering if all this walking is contributing to any weight loss, the answer is not really, because ITALIANS! There is no option to refuse a morsel of food. You have to eat.

Tonight we had mussels with linguini. RIDICULOUSLY DELICIOUS. Prepared with love by young Italian men who want to just watch you eat and enjoy your food.

Eating with the Italians is a communal event every single time for every single meal. It's an experience. Even a little snack in the middle of the day is a moment to stop, eat, talk, share, be together.

The dinner party included entertainment which was performed in Italian/Spanish. Mikele and Jessica wrote a song and sang it to us after dinner. It was to honor those leaving the trail to go back to regular life. A ballad of love and admiration for how far we have come personally and physically. We all bawled.

I spent a lot of solo time on the Camino today and it does get a bit boring so I listen to podcasts sometimes. I just realized that I have Spotify premium, and so I listened to music for the first time.
No kidding, this was the first song that came on:

I don't know where I'm going
But I sure know where I've been
Hanging on the promises
And songs of yesterday
And I've made up my mind
I ain't wasting no more time
But here I go again
Though I keep searching for the answer
I never seem to find what I'm looking for
Oh Lord, I pray
You give me the strength to carry on
'Cause I know what it means
To walk along the lonely street of dreams

—"Here I Go Again" by White Snake

(Air guitar solo with my trekking poles...)

Day 11: Today I Ate Wheat Seeds

Belorado to Atapuerca
20.3 miles (WHAT?!)

I don't even know how this is possible, but I think we walked over 20 miles today.

So this is how it happened. We decided to walk to Ages which was 4.2km farther than our destination. We wanted a jump start on tomorrow, because tomorrow we walk to Burgos, a big city where we might take a rest day, might not.

My fave 13-year-old pilgrim, Julia, kept me PUMPED for the last 2 miles. She loves 80s music, so we sang DON'T STOP BELIEVING and SWEET CHILD OF MINE at the top of our lungs.

Once we get to Burgos we will pass into an area known as the Meseta which is going to be a ten-day walk through...well, nothing. A lot of people skip this area because it's so

Julia is 13 years old and I have never heard her complain one single time.

harsh. Google it. I am not skipping it because I am committed to walking this whole trail.

So we arrived to Ages and I am really tired and just DONE walking. There are three albergues in town and NONE OF THEM HAVE A KITCHEN! Mikele and Rosario cook every night. Last night we had lemon chicken, zucchini fried in olive oil and topped with salt, pasta with some kind of magic sauce, salad, fresh melons, cookies, and chocolate. And of course that supper fresh baguette bread.

So after much discussion (in Italian so I can only pick up a few words like *cucina* which means kitchen) we decided to walk an additional almost two miles to come here because there is a kitchen where they can cook. I know, it seems easier to just pop into a cafe to get food but have you ever had fresh Italian food cooked WITH LOVE from Italian men who only want to feed people?

The Camino looked like this today.

The other day Rosario culled some asparagus and onions from some of the farms we passed through. This is an ancient and accepted tradition on the Camino for farmers to plant gardens for the pilgrims close to the trail. He used this in our dinner. He's also picked up cherries, berries, and other vegetables. He only takes what he needs to feed his Camino family.

Today I ate wheat seeds. There are miles and miles of wheat fields that we walk through. What you do is find a sprig that is dry, no green. Break off the top and just pull off the seeds into your hand. Crush them around a little to loosen the chaff and then gently blow the chaff away so all you have are the little seeds. It's looks like super healthy cereal you'd buy at Whole Foods, then put the seeds in your mouth and let them get soft. They are chewy and delicious. I ate kind of a lot.

Weird enchanted stuff was going on all over the trail today: warm and cold areas, a section with hundreds of butterflies, swarms of bees drinking out of puddles, black forests like in Germany, free range cows just waking by with their judgmental glances and musical bells, picnic areas with totem poles, ferns that grown from the ground like they do in Oregon, rain, sun, warm, cold, blue skies, and grey skies.

This wide path had TONS of rock messages for pilgrims. Arrows are popular rock formations. So are words of encouragement spelled out with rocks like KEEP GOING or LOVE or BUEN CAMINO. Whoever takes the time to make those rock messages....thank you.

As I lay in my bottom bunk bed with my feet propped up on a pile of clothes (pulled my hammy yesterday), I can hear the Italians chopping vegetables and heating olive oil for dinner preparations. It's 7:15 but we won't actually eat until after 9pm.

I have no idea what I'm doing. I never feel like I've got it together or that I have figured out this Camino thing or if I'm doing this right. All I do is get up every morning and start walking.

One thing I did not expect was the extreme temperature differences on the Camino. I expected it to be hot, and it is, but sometimes it gets cold in the morning, especially in the mountains. On this particular morning when we began walking it was 43 degrees outside.

Day 12: Random Dogs

July 2, 2017
Atapuerca to Burgos
Approximately 13-14 miles

Well, I got lost today for the first time. It was only an hour, but still. AN EXTRA HOUR OF WALKING! No thank you. Thank GOD I have Jules with me who knows how to do a pin drop on her phone, AND she can speak intermediate level Spanish.

On my way back from getting lost. Atapuerca far in the distance.

I don't know if I'm getting stronger or the hills are a little less intimidating, but I managed to climb another "alto" and I wasn't completely dead when I got to the top. We are slowly making our way into the center region of Spain. Those charming medieval cities are behind us.

Burgos is a very modern city that looks like it's been through some hard times. Abandoned buildings, lots of graffiti, and for the first time I've seen trash in the streets.

We entered the outskirts of the city and then had to walk four to five miles to reach our albergue. Today is Sunday and everything is closed, but people are out and about enjoying the beautiful day. This is a departure from the small, rural villages where siesta times are strictly observed and I see and hear no one during siesta.

Heading toward Burgos.

The best thing about Burgos: the dogs! Everyone has a dog here. Big ones, little ones, fat, skinny, cute, ugly, pure breeds, mutts. Every kind of dog you can imagine, and they are all out today.

Which brings me to another interesting tidbit of information because it happened again today: I can't tell you how many times I'm walking through a village early in the morning and here comes a random dog walking down the road going to some unknown destination. Like work, maybe? One of my favorite things about the Camino is probably the animal life I get to experience. I spend all day outside walking through farm country. I'm becoming keenly aware of the sights, sounds, and smells of animals. There has not been one morning that I did not hear a rooster.

I stood in a wheat field today.

I walked through a wheat field today. That was insanely fun for some reason. It was a short cut that got us back on the Camino and heading in the right direction. How did we know were going the right direction? We saw people in the distance with backpacks. Pilgrims. Just follow them. That's what I do.

Tomorrow is going to be a long day and I need to go in search of provisions.

Jules and I had Spanish tapas for dinner tonight, I drank a glass of wine and it was all I could do to stay up past 8:30pm.

Feeling happy in Burgos.

71

Day 13: Ave Maria

Burgos to Hontanas
19.5 miles
200 miles total
300 miles to Santiago (this is probably completely inaccurate)

Today I woke up with an awful attitude. The attitude started the night before when I was out eating tapas and having a beautiful moment with my Camino family. At 8:15 pm I just hit a wall, and it was all I could do to walk back to the albergue and drop into bed. I already made plans to get out the door by 6:00 am to try to beat the heat, and the thought of getting up and walking, AGAIN, just made me pissy. Leaving the city of Burgos left me feeling even more blah. It was too suburbia with broken down buildings, roads with cars, trashy streets, and not at all the Camino I left behind.

I was so happy when I got to a little village with its super narrow streets, two story buildings, and old, ancient, sacred architecture. Walking through these old villages I can't help but feel comfortable and protected. Like nothing bad can happen to me. Like the spirits of the Knights Templar are watching over me as I walk down the cobbled streets.   There was a building that looked like an old one room schoolhouse. Even though I was determined to reach my destination early, I knew I had to check it out. It turned out to be a small, old, and very charming little church. I try to stop at as many churches as possible. They always have a beautiful stamp for my credential, and they are cool and relaxing. In the corner, a dear, old lady was diligently and professionally giving stamps. I instantly fell in love with her. She stamped my credential and then put a square piece of paper over it so the ink wouldn't spread. Then she placed a little necklace over my neck with a pendant of the

The sweetest old church lady I've ever met.

Virgin Mary. She held my hand and said a little prayer, and she told me that Mary would protect me on my journey. She spoke only Spanish, but I somehow knew exactly what she said. There was a radio in the church that was playing one of the most beautiful renditions of Ave Maria. I just stood and listened to the whole thing. Boom. I'm back on the Camino with a renewed spirit and soul.

My pilgrim's credential, which I get stamped at various places like albergues, bars, cafes, churches, stores. When I arrive in Santiago, I will have to present this as proof of my pilgrimage before I receive my official Pilgrim's Certification.

After the church, I plowed through the miles. For the majority of the day, like 15 miles, it was wheat fields and blue skies. Nothing else. Except swarms and swarms of butterflies that went on for miles and miles.

I switched up my foot routine. I put on my shoes and socks and just started walking. No tape, no Compeed®, no liners, just go. Somehow it worked for me today.

Also today I discovered the power of music. I listened to my I Heart Radio app, where there is a station prepared for me based on my preferences. Here are a few of the artists chosen for me:

- George Michael
- Culture Club
- Phil Collins
- Prince
- Yaz
- Depeche Mode
- Bruno Mars
- Elton John
- James Brown
- Fleetwood Mac

I'm such an 80's child!

Wheat fields and blue skies, 80 degrees with a little breeze.

I followed this pilgrim for about three hours. He also took a photo with the farmer. When he found out I was an American he made the farmer take a picture of us. He said "Oh! American! Cowboy! This is probably the 4th time I've been referred to as a cowboy so I very politely informed him that I'm a "cowgirl." I think he said he was Romanian.

75

I took a selfie with a farmer today. I told him, "no hablo Español," and I'm pretty sure he said to me that if I'm in Spain I should be speaking Spanish.

And finally, a little laundry in Hontanas. One of the best things about some of these albergues is when they offer laundry service. IT'S SO WORTH IT! It takes so much time to do laundry and it's the last thing I want to do at the end of a long, dirty day.

There are several conversations in several languages going on within my hearing range right now and I love it.

I've never walked 20 miles in my life!

Happiness is the shoe room. Keep that stink quarantined!

Day 14: I Didn't Eat a Hamburger Today

Hontanas to Boadilla
17 miles

Fourth of July. Independence Day in the United States.

If you are considering going on the adventure of a lifetime and want to walk 500 miles across Spain, do me a favor and do everything the exact opposite of what I've done. I'm SUCH AN AMATEUR and it has finally caught up with me.

No holiday for us, we walk because we are pilgrims and that's what we do.

what I've done. I'm SUCH AN AMATEUR and it has finally caught up with me.

Believe it or not, I have to take a bus tomorrow to a pilgrim's hospital AND I need to get new shoes. It's mandatory or I won't make it.

The first day over the Pyrenees was awful (refer to *Day 1: Today was HORRIBLE*) and I got a horrible sunburn which I've been told was second degree burns. (YES! I

This is me now. This is what I have become. This was an effort to avoid bugs, but they managed to sneak in through the sides of my sunglasses and get in my eyes.

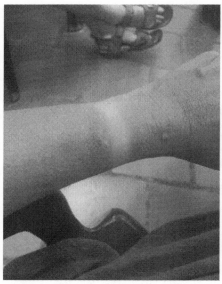

Really gross sunburn

wore sunscreen!) It's getting worse so I need to make sure I get it on the path to healing.

Plus, I know you are sick and tired of hearing about my feet, but the reality of getting up and hiking for seven-11 hours a day is just catching up with me. I'm walking with Jules who is a yogi and expert hiker, a 21-year-old Division I swimmer, and I've kept up with her for 14 days, but I need to be smarter if I'm going to finish this.

I'm not feeling one drop of guilt for having to leave the trail for a day or two. I'm traveling with another pilgrim whose blisters are so horrific I worry her Camino might be over. We are going together and will meet up with our friends at the end of the day.

I've heard that some pilgrims I started with tapped out after the first day. Others have taken days off or take a bus to the next stage. Some ship their packs or walk half the stage and get a ride for the remainder. This is all perfectly normal and acceptable.

Everyone has to do his or her own Camino. The goal is to make it to Santiago in one piece.

I will never get tired of these village roads.

View from the village

Day 15: I Stood in a River Today

Boadilla to Carrion (car ride)

Just standing in a river.

Day 16: Zero Shade

*Carrión de los Condes to Terradillos de los Templarios
16.7 miles*

HALFWAY TO SANTIAGO!

So cool that this little village (population 80) used to be
a stronghold for the Knights Templar. Now there are
two albergues, a couple of farms, and that's it.

*Such a sweet village on the
Camino.*

We are making our way
across an area known
as the Meseta. It's
basically a featureless
landscape with zero
shade. I was worried
about today because
there was a ten-mile
stretch with nothing,
zilch, nada. Just wheat
fields and blue skies.
It's important to get
through this EARLY so
the sun is not beating
down on my soul and
zapping all of my
strength and energy.

Snack break with zero shade.

The Camino spirits were sooooooo good to us today because it was cool, breezy, cloud covered and FLAT. Before you know it, five miles done, then ten, then boom, arrived by 1:30pm. Shower, laundry, nap, pilgrim's meal, Facebook blog, sleep, up at 5am, repeat.

The good news is that the next few days are flat. The bad news is that we are expecting rain, which means mud and wet shoes. There just isn't much going on other than putting in the miles to get through.

Things I have witnessed on the Camino:
- Two Frenchmen sitting on the side of the path for a rest offered me a prune as I walked by. It was delicious. Later they passed me as they were singing.
- Old men hanging out in their village just pilgrim watching (kind of like watching mall walkers).
- A couple of guys using rocks to crack open almonds picked off a tree.
- Sheep herds being led by a single dog.
- Fields of poppies
- Hearing five to ten languages a day and somehow understanding what's being said.
- Meeting people who are on their second and third Camino.

The Camino repeaters all return for the exact same reason: the people.

I have heard many people say they would walk the Camino for the rest of their life. They never want to leave this trail. Everyone who is here has a common goal or feeling, and it's palpable. Even though we are all completely different we are all connected through this experience. This rarely happens in everyday life.

Kind of like a hobbit cave, but not really.

Today I spent a lot of time thinking about the day I'll walk into Santiago. I'm not one of those people who wants to do this forever. I don't even think I'll ever want to do it again.

I was listening to this song when the Frenchmen were feeding me a prune:

It's not in the way you hold me
It's not in the way you say you care
It's not in the way you've been treating my friends
It's not in the way you stayed till the end
It's not in the way you look
or the things you'll say you do

— "Hold the Line" by Toto

The rock formations never get old. They just pop up on the road and go on and on. So inspiring.

Love.

Kevin from Holland. All his clothes are in the wash so he came to dinner wearing his sleep sack.

Blister wicking with Jules and her headlamp.

Day 17: Rain Nap

Terradillos to Calzadilla
15 miles

Rain. Sun. Wind. More rain. Wind. Mud. Dirt.

We were so tired this morning. Like walking-dead feet-dragging tired. Stopped at the first café we came to for café con leche and rest.

Made it to halfway point by 10:30am. Snack, groceries, bank, and pharmacy for sixies, milagro, and sleeping pills. All natural! Don't judge!

Jules taking a Camino nap.

Re-packed our bags and then Jules and I began looking for a place to lay down and take a little siesta before walking the last 10k.

12:00: Find a park, warm breeze, sun, lay out rain gear, use packs as pillows, pull buff over eyes, fall immediately to sleep.
12:15: Massive wind wakes us up, dark clouds coming in.

12:16: Grab our stuff, throw on our rain gear, and run to get cover under a bridge.

12:16-12:30: Stand under bridge and watch rain come down in buckets.

12:31: Rain lets up, crawl out from cover, get back on the Camino.

12:45: Run into Kevin from Holland who has been traveling in the rain with friends. Friends seek cover, Kevin does not.

Not my fave.

12:50: Rain becomes real gross and we regret everything in life.

12:55: Kevin passes me singing, "Shine Bright Like a Diamond".

12:55-1:30: Rain is even grosser, soaking wet and miserable.

1:31: Rain turns into sun shower.

1:45: Rain stops, sun comes out, peel off rain gear and hang it off backpack.

2:00: Find a spot to change soaking wet shoes to trail sandals.

2:45: Eat two granola bars.

3:30: Arrive at destination.

A Camino rainbow.

Day 18: Solitude

Calzadilla to Mansilla
17 miles today
Miles to go: 235.1
Days to Santiago: 14 (OMG! Almost there!)

The Meseta. The good thing about this section of Spain is that it is fast and flat. The bad thing about it is that it's kind of boring.

People are few and far between. Unless you are walking with a specific group, you might not see many people unless you're in a cafe or albergue. As a matter of fact, tons of people skip this section because it's so blah. But not the bikers! This is the perfect biking section, so it's common to have them whiz by wearing their neon colors and geometric shapes. Such a contrast to the landscape.

I remember my biggest fear was finding a bed every night and so far that had been a non-issue. Every night beds are available in the municipal albergues and they are usually only €6 or €7 a night. And they're totally decent! I will likely never stay in a hotel again. I

The Camino looked like this all day.

like the communal atmosphere and I like the fact I can chill by myself and no one bothers me.

Staying in an albergue requires a complete relinquishing of personal comfort barriers that I think most of my friends couldn't handle. For example:
- Boys and girls use the same bathroom for everything including potty and showers.
- Boys and girls sleep in the same rooms.
- I'm usually sharing bunk rooms with 12-100 people depending on the albergue.
- There's always a curfew so doors are locked at 10:00 pm, lights out at 10:30 pm.

But on the bright side:
- No one walks around naked! (Well, almost.)
- It's day 18 and I've managed to score a bottom bunk every night.
- There's almost always a kitchen with people cooking and lots of leftovers.
- Sometimes there are ten-15 conversations going on in as many languages.

Some albergues are hundreds of years old and some are brand new. Occasionally I have to wash and dry my clothes by hand, which is so awkward for me. I have no idea what I'm doing. I try to imagine how Laura did it on episodes of "Little House on the Prairie" or other period dramas from TV. The key is to get here early enough to get them washed and hung out to dry before the sun goes down. Many times, I start the day with my clothes hanging off my pack to dry. The worst part is trying to squeeze out all the water. I never knew the glory of the spin cycle.

Got caught in another rainstorm today. So gross. My feet are even grosser, but blisters are currently either healing or numb. Tomorrow we will reach the city of León.

Day 19: Burger King

Mansilla to León
11.2 miles

You might think that there is no possible way that every day on the Camino can be special. Come on, I'm going to be walking this thing for over 30 days. Some days have to be just...you know...walking.

The whole day looked like this.

That was my day today. The most exciting thing happened before 8am when I watched the running of the bulls on a TV in a small café.

After that I saw a few cute animals. It got kind of hot, so I was sweaty. My feet hurt really bad, but then they went numb. I kept walking.

Get up that hill, biker dude ringing your bell as you pass by.

At about 10:00 am Jules and I shared an amazing tomato, egg and cheese sandwich. And we had a short day, only like 13 miles. That's NOTHING compared to some of our 20+ days. Kind of boring. I was bummed I had nothing to blog about.

And then, right when we got into the heart of this beautiful walled city, MAGIC happened.

WE FOUND A BURGER KING AND ATE OUR FACES OFF!

OMG! I had a whopper and it was so delicious. EXACTLY like home. Not like European fast food, like real American junk food. AND HEINZ KETCHUP! THE REAL DEAL! PITTSBURGH IN THE HOUSE!

Burger King.

Even health-food Jules was loving fast food on the Camino.

For those of you who haven't eaten European fast food, it's such a disappointment, it's the same but different. Always that curry ketchup with the fries. Not the same. THIS WAS THE SAME! It's the little things.

Made it to our albergue in the heart of the old city. Tourists pay big money to stay in locations like this. But because we are official pilgrims, we only paid €6 a night.

Day 20: Breakfast Tapas

León
REST DAY!
No walking! No backpack! NADA!

This morning we had to leave our albergue by 8:00 am so they could clean it and turn it over for the next batch of pilgrims. Even though we got kicked out, we still got to sleep in until 7:30 am! Luxury!

Breakfast tapas.

So off we go in search of a cafe where we can chill until check in at 11:00 am. There is this thing in Spain where THEY GIVE YOU FOOD if you order a drink. A cup of cafe con leche for €1.50 came with a FREE HOMEMADE PASTRY! Seriously!

While sitting at the counter eating breakfast tapas, a young girl came in for her first day of walking. (Many people begin the Camino in León.) She is doing a different route through the mountains that leads her up north before heading west to Santiago. She left her fleece on the bus and was distressed about having to wait for stores to open at 10:30 am to buy something to keep her warm. I just kicked into mom mode and gave her my super deluxe REI shirt because I couldn't stand the thought of her being cold. So many people have swooped in to save me on this trail. From giving me food to threading blisters to helping me sort my backpack, standing guard over my things, waiting for me to make sure I'm not lost or scared, and most importantly, being there as a friend when I really needed one. It was my turn to pay it forward. I'll miss my super deluxe REI shirt, but I can always get another one, right?

Bye, REI shirt. Jessie needs you more than I do.

Jules and I did a little walking tour of this beautiful city. Google León...you'll be blow away.

A Gaudi in León.

We walked over a 400 year-old mosaic.

We visited the cathedral for the compulsory audio tour, did some window shopping, ran into friends (always the best thing ever to see people you know in a random European city), and then we did something even more incredible.

We took a siesta.

Spain SHUTS DOWN for siesta from 1:30 to 5:30 pm, so there is really no other option.

Makeout sesh with Tyrian Lannister. Don't be jelly!

Last night I had to say goodbye to my two favorite Italian sons, Mikele and Marco. This was emotional.

I met Mikele on Day 1 and really got to know him on Day 4, which was his birthday. He cooked dinner for a group of about 15 people and just sat back to watch everyone eat.

He said he was worried that he might have to spend his birthday by himself, but instead he was enjoying having dinner with a group of wonderful people. He was so happy! I love this kid!

He cooked so many dinners for our group.

Every morning he would kiss me on the cheek like his mama. I looked out for him and he looked out for me.

My Camino son.

Mikele and Marco, my Italian sons.

Like so many people you meet on the Camino there is a beginning and end. Like an ebb and flow of passing in and out of each other's lives. You know you may never see them again, but their existence in your life is carved into your soul forever. It's the spirit of the Camino. The Camino family.

My last day with some Camino family members new and old.

I got a new pullover to wear on cold mornings. It's not my super deluxe REI shirt but it's a cute Nike three quarter zip that was on sale.

Day 21: GIRL FIGHT!

León to Villadangos
13.6 miles: EASY
12 days to go
Tomorrow is going to be a rough day with 17+ miles in the heat.

Today's walk was bleak. After leaving the walled city of León we traveled all day through broken down towns, truck stops, wilted and dead crops, lots of trash on the road and trail, and a whole lot of nothing exciting. Boring.

I love a fountain with water coming out of its mouth.

Let's move on to the good stuff.

The real story is that there was an incident last night at my albergue involving my friend, Jules.

This is the first albergue I've stayed in with separate rooms for guys and girls. We know this because we stayed here the night before. No big deal, all good. The common theme among all the municipal and parochial albergues, which are almost always run by nuns and volunteers, is that you must be in by 10:00 pm and lights out at 10:30 pm. No talking, lights off.

But people are ALWAYS using headlamps to take care of business because if you arrive later in the day you need to eat, do laundry, and prepare for the next day. 10:00 pm gets here early! That's also usually when it starts to cool down. And when you're in a room with 20-100 people, it's just not realistic to expect everyone to be on the same page. Many nights I go to sleep with lights on, people still milling about. It's the way of life in hostels. You know this going in. Plus, it's €5-6 a night! So cheap! *

(*Note: I calculated that it's going to cost €72 for rooming from now until Santiago. That's 12 days of rooming with showers, laundry facilities, spotty Wi-Fi, usually a kitchen, and more.)

Let me give you some background info on Jules. Expert level hiker. Hiked Yosemite. (HARD!) Yoga and mindfulness teacher in a public school in San Francisco. (I know, dream job!) Extremely well-studied in all things cool like homeopathic treatments, essential oils, meditation, acupuncture, eastern philosophy.

The epitome of C-A-L-M.

Kindness to the Nth degree.

A truly spiritual soul who only wants to give and empower people's lives.

She eats the good kale.

So this is how it went down:

9:45-10:00 pm: Jules is quietly doctoring her feet. She has a system that works for her blisters and she is meticulous with foot preparations. Absolutely critical at this stage of the Camino.

10:05 pm: Crazy Lady gets up out of her bed and puts her face right next to Jules and screams at her that it's bedtime and the lights must be turned off. Jules politely asks her to back off and that she is almost done with her feet prep. Another woman, Sweet Christian Lady, says, "We are all good Christian women here and we should get along." Jules says, "Wow, someone really needs this Camino because she is just a mean person with no compassion."

10:05-10:15 pm: It's completely silent. Jules is almost done with her feet. I have just completed my Facebook update and laid down to sleep. Crazy Lady gets up again and gets directly in Jules face and starts screaming LOUDLY at her. She then walks over to the light switch and shuts off the lights. Very awkward, other ladies are all awake now, totally uncomfortable. Jules only needs five minutes to do her thing. She put on her headlamp with the softest light setting to finish her task.

10:20 pm: Crazy Lady jumps out of bed, runs over to Jules screaming, pulls her headlamp off her head and grabs her arm. I jump out of my bed for the assist and block this woman with my arm. She tries to shove me out of the way. She's maybe 4'10", grey hair, missing front teeth, really bad breath, and screaming at me in very broken English. I detect a French accent.

Come on you guys, I'm a high school teacher. I can handle a tiny conflict even though I'm half asleep. I turned on my teacher voice and told her to get back in bed. I think I even said something about not being allowed to put your hands on other people.

Meanwhile, Sweet Christian Lady ran to get help from the workers. Here comes the 4'9" head nun, who is the one in charge of the whole place. She is trying to figure out what is going on. All the ladies are awake at this point. Christian Lady tells the nun that Crazy Lady had verbally harassed her and others the previous day. Jules and I grab our things and move to another room while the nun informs Crazy Lady that lights out are not until 10:30. There is even talk of perhaps calling the *polizia*.

Jules finished taping her feet, we settled ourselves into new beds and sleep like babies for the rest of the night.

Camino sisters resting on the Camino a few hours down the trail from León.

Day 22: Wear More Sunscreen

Villadangos to Astorga
18.45 miles

And just like that, my beloved Camino is back. I could not be more thankful for cobblestone roads, ancient villages with artful bridges, winding our way down narrow streets, greeting the locals, and finding that pull of the Camino spirit.

Centuries-old bridges make me so HAPPY!

Can't help but feel inspired by the Camino and the architecture.

They just don't make water towers like they used to.

Goodbye, Meseta. You're kind of icky, but I get it. Not all roads through life are beautiful and inspiring, but in the end we get to where we need to be.

I see the color purple. Every. Single. Day.

Today was an R. Kelly-Boys to Men-Mariah Carey-Kendrick Lamar-George Michael-Bruno

Hello, cobblestone streets. I've missed you.

Mars-Taylor Swift-Prince-Fleetwood Mac playlist kind of day.

I was so happy walking today that I almost ran. Hills! They used to give me flashbacks of Day 1 walking over the Pyrenees. (See *Day 1: Today was HORRIBLE!*) But not today. I flew through 17.5 miles like a breeze.

Let's talk about feet! A lot of the large city municipal albergues offer services for pilgrims like massages, medical care, AND blister treatment. My feet have been champs for the past five to six days, but there's still a lot of grossness going on down there. So I got an appointment to see a student podiatrist to get my feet scraped and treated. These services are free (or small donativo) and totally amazing. I could go into detail about that, but I won't because it's just gross.

I love getting messages from people offering encouragement and asking questions. Some of my friends are really inspired to walk the Camino and I absolutely want everyone to do it.

I came into this thinking I had done the necessary preparations and enough training to get me through. WRONG! There is no way to prepare or train for this.

The Camino makes you face every fear you've ever had and deal with it directly. What are you afraid of the most? Is it personal safety, getting lost, getting hurt, extreme pain, emotional stuff, isolation, leaving something behind, running out of food, running out of water, bed bugs, crazy people, the heat, the cold, the wind, losing track of friends, being alone, not being able to sleep, giving up every ounce of privacy, and the worst fear of all…not making it to Santiago. All of it is here and everyone goes through it. And we all get up the next day and continue walking.

My ONLY regret is not wearing more sunscreen.

When the Camino calls, you will know. There will be no denying that you need to do this. There is no age or physical requirement to do this. All you need is the will to get up every day and walk.

At the entrance to Astorga this little boy was offering cold drinks to pilgrims for a donativo. He had little plastic cups and when we finished drinking, he sprinted to the garbage can to throw the used cup away and then sprinted back to handle business. I asked him what he was going to do with all the money

he made this summer and he said he was saving up for a school trip to England so of course I basically gave him all my money. A future traveler…be still my heart.

A Camino fundraiser.

I love these narrow-street villages.

Cobblestone roads make me so unbelievably happy.

Day 23: The Story of the Canadian Masseuse

Astorga to Foncebadón
about 17.5 miles (ish, prob a little more, like doing a half marathon then walking up 55 flights of stairs, only not stairs, more like a hill with rocks, only not rocks, more like boulders)
9 or 10 days to Santiago

Up early and ready to hike up some mountains.

The pain was located in that part of the shoulder that is not easily accessible by one's own hand. It was a pinch. Deep breath, feel it. Relax the shoulders, still feel it. Adjust the pack, pain goes away momentarily but then take 10 steps and it's still there. The pack was heavy so there was a shifting pattern that occurred for at least 10k. Use the thumb straps to hold the pack just so as to not cause pain. It's still there. All attempts at mindfulness and focusing on the elbow which has no pain are thwarted by the pain. After 22 days of walking six-11 hours per day while carrying a 15-18-pound pack this is reality. Get to next village, take a sixie, try to stretch and try to get through this pinching that is just now starting to crawl up into the neck because why have just shoulder pain when there's so much more that can be hurting.

Cafe in the distance with the ubiquitous plastic chairs. Throw down pack, sit down, dig for sixie and try to imagine life without pain. On the verge of tears. It really hurts the bad kind of hurt.

Friends arrive and take immediate control of the situation.

The traveling trio included a masseuse. Not just any masseuse, but a Canadian one. A Canadian masseuse who is in such high demand that her clients fly her all over Canada and America for her services. A Canadian masseuse who is also a yogi with the kind of knowledge about things like how certain muscles are attached to certain organs and the massage is more about releasing toxins and cleansing the mind, body, and spirit. The kind of massage that touches on former life stuff and other internal processes that are only known by masters of meditation and yoga.

There were moments of blinding lights coming out of the brain during this 15-minute shoulder massage. Deep breath in, let it out, breathe some more, actual tears, relax your head in my hand while I adjust your spine, make a little temple on the head and let out all the bad juju.

Later on the mountain, the American was climbing and the wind blew away of lot of feelings that went into the air and got mixed up with the dirt and trees and grass. It took some of that bad juju that was released from the body by that Canadian masseuse and mixed it with all the other rubbish left by ancient pilgrims who walked over this little mountain.

In return for this cleansing, the American bought a €1 shell necklace from an old lady who was selling trinkets out of her home. She gave it to the Canadian masseuse who loved it so much she cried.

I saw a rock today with the message, "Life is wine."

I can see the valley below where we came from, and the mountains in the distance are what we will walk over in three days.

There are steep hills with those ever-present boulders that continue to shred my feet.

Three camingas with our three best-friend-for-life shells that I got from the old trinket lady for €1.

Day 24: Duct Tape

Forncebadon to Ponferrada
Long hot 17+ mile day

I started the morning in crisis because my CamelBak water bag sprung a leak and drenched the bottom of my pack. Wet stuff is a non-issue. Not having a handy water supply is a HUGE ISSUE.

It's not handy or convenient to put a water bottle in one of the pockets of my pack because I have to remove my pack to reach it. Nevertheless, I had to have water so I ended up with a 2-liter bottle totally out of reach. And even worse, I was super grouchy about it. I needed a new CamelBak or duct tape and the last place to get anything like that was one village back in Astorga.

The morning brought me to La Cruz de Ferro, which I have been waiting to see for a long time. Since before the school year ended, I've been planning on visiting this spot. It's a very simple cross where pilgrims take time to reflect and reconnect with the purpose of their journey. It is then customary to leave a stone as a token of love or blessings. Some will carry a stone from home to this location and use it as a way to symbolically unload a burden. I didn't have a burden to unload, just a token of love.

My rock at La Cruz de Ferro.

I have been carrying this rock for a long time, even before I came here. This little thing was extra special because my student Kristina painted it for me.

I left the rock at the base of the cross rather than the top, mostly because I wanted to show it off. It worked! Before I left, I caught a random dude taking a picture of it.

I walked away and had to fight the urge to run back and grab it. I'm tempted to ask some friends who are traveling a day behind me to get it and bring it to Santiago for me.

I spent so much time today thinking about my girls, Haley and Izzy. I miss them terribly and I know they're following me, but I need to have hours long conversations with them.

The whole time I've been walking I've also been carrying the secret that two babies are coming into my family. Izzy is pregnant and so is my brother and sister-in-law. I found out exactly two weeks before I departed for Europe about Izzy and my only solace is that her and Haley are in constant contact. Big sister looking out for little sister. My greatest accomplishment. The night I arrived to SJPP I got news of Scott and Stephanie's pregnancy. Two babies who will be born only one month apart. It's impossible not to cry when I think of it.

The trail today was really intense. Steep downhills into canyons over solid rock and limestone. Plus, it got crazy hot.

I discovered this really cool thing. My cargo shorts have pockets that can hold a bottle of water. So utilitarian I've become!

I spent the entire day by myself and it was so relaxing that I decided that I'm striking out on my own again tomorrow.

The Camino looked like this today.

About two kilometers from my destination for the day, I crossed a bridge and I heard someone call out to me. She asked if I wanted to come rest in the shade for a few minutes. As a matter of fact, I did. She was about my age, maybe older, traveling with her brother as a kind of memorial walk in honor of their father who died the previous year. Americans from Northern California around Gilroy. The Garlic Capital of the World. Her eyes lit up when I told her I was from Chico. When you travel all over the world and meet someone who knows about Chico and they find out you're from Chico you get instant street credibility.

She had duct tape so I could mend my Camelbak.

The Camino provides.

Day 25: Reinhardt

Molinaseca to Vega de Valcarce
9.5 miles (10.5 miles in a car)
Preparing to climb O'Cebreiro tomorrow
4,297 feet!

OMG, I'm so happy today! I'm finally reunited with a major portion of my Camino family, people who I've known and walked with since Roncesvalles.

Another Camino love story: the couple who runs the albergue where I'm staying tonight met and fell in love on the Camino eight years ago. She is Italian and he is from Chile. You can't find two more lovely people on the entire Camino.

Tonight, at our communal dinner, I met Reinhardt from Germany who has been walking for 75 days. He is 70 years old. He walked out of his front door in Germany because it was cheaper than buying a plane ticket. Today I got to share a meal with him.

He has had ZERO blisters. He said that he

Happy to be back with my favorite 13-year old, Julia.

My honorary cousin, Reinhardt.

has so much to be thankful for: married for 48 years, three children, seven grandchildren, his health, his life. He is walking the Camino to celebrate all of this. Along the way he has met hundreds of people, he has slept in a different bed, sometimes even a floor, for 75 days. He has never made a reservation and just walks until he feels that's enough. He has slept on church floors in France and paid nothing. He once had to pay €120 for a room because that was the only room left in town. Mostly he stays in albergues that cost €5-9, which is what I do. He said that every day on the Camino is completely different. Even if it's just the weather or the food. I talked to him about my German roots and then decided that we are officially cousins.

We are getting so close to Santiago. There are old wine presses and vineyards all along the trial today.

I will be in Santiago by next Saturday.

Day 26: Climbing O'Cebreiro

Vega de Valcarce to Fonfría
15 miles-ish

Up the mountain and down the mountain.

I was more prepared for this hike than I expected. First of all, most of the uphill was in the cool morning and it was nowhere near the trauma of walking over the Pyrenees.

I was so happy when Reinhardt got caught up in my walking orbit this morning. I got to complete the final

Celebrating our climb with a nip of wine.

ascent with him and walk all the way to the top to see the views. He carries a plastic bottle with wine and a small plastic cup so our little group of four had a nip to celebrate our victory. He is walking 10k past our stopping point today and the sad reality is that I may never see him again. I feel so lucky to know him.

The highest point on the mountain, above the clouds.

I saw a rock today that said, "Let the wisdom of uncertainty guide you."

My "hills are alive with the sound of music" moment.

At one point today we were shocked and confused because someone left raspberries for passing pilgrims and we couldn't understand how someone could be so wonderful.

Our albergue for the night is located in a mountain farm village with approximately six to seven buildings. It's SMALL. But this albergue is HIGH CLASS.

This is what a €10 private albergue gets you rather than the €6 municipal:

- Showers that stay on, rather than push button showers that you have to restart every 30 seconds and have no control over the water temperature.
- Lights that stay on, rather than shut off after five seconds of no movement so you have to wave your hands and jump around to get them to turn back on.
- A plug next to your bunk, so you can charge your phone while lying in bed cruising the internet.
- Decent Wi-Fi.
- Separate male/female bathrooms. But still a common bunk room.
- Indoor and outdoor lounge areas.
- Pilgrims meals served communal style, for usually around €6-7. Totally worth it.

I have to admit, I really don't want to get up and walk tomorrow. I'm ready to be done and it's so close but there are still six more days of walking.

The routine is wearing on me. Getting up early, walking for six to nine hours, the heat, bunk beds, flies all the time everywhere, laundry, shower in primitive conditions, always feeling

My little €10 albergue is so dang cute.

tired, sore, hot, gross, hungry, thirsty, emotional, stoic, homesick.

I'm glad it's ending soon. I can't wait to be a civilian again.

Some members of my Camino fam including 13-year-old Julia, me, Julies, Emily and Enda from Ireland.

Everyone should hang out with 21-year-olds. To me, Sara and Emily will remain 21 for all eternity. These girls got me through some tough days.

Made it to Galicia! The last region on this pilgrimage!

Day 27: Bottom Bunk

Fonfria to Sarria
20 miles

Currently laying in my bottom
bunk in the city of Sarria.
Trying not to think about the
heat. 100k from Santiago.

It is from this city that a
pilgrim MUST walk in order to
receive an official "Credencial
del Peregrino" in the city of
Santiago. A pilgrim must walk
and gather official
documentation for the last
100km in the form of stamps

*Feeling like a boss with
the backpack I got for
€37 in Logroño.*

on your pilgrim's passport. Even if you walked all the
way from Paris, Germany or beyond, if you have to
take a bus or other form of transportation through one
of the stages in the last 100km, your pilgrimage never
happened in the eyes of the church. It won't be
marked in the historical records.

I realize this is a journey about personal reflection and
growth. It's about clearing out the layers of soot that
has built up on your soul and leaving all that dirt
behind on the trail. It's about taking steps into being
the person that you are...not who you used to be or
want to be. It's about conquering fear and anxiety and

becoming a giver rather than a taker. All of this and more cannot be recorded on a piece of paper.

But you know I WANT MY PILGRIM'S CREDENTIAL! I will crawl on my hands and knees down every last inch of this trail to get it!

So, because of this requirement there are HUNDREDS of people who begin this pilgrimage right here in Sarria, walk for six to seven days, and get the same credential that I'm getting. It's ok, I've accepted this, but obviously I have a bit of an attitude about it.

About 10km from arriving in Sarria the crowds started. Solitude time is O-V-E-R. There are buses full of tourists, lots of buses, which drop off groups of 40-50 to walk a little bit, get the mandatory two stamps per day on their credentials, and then they all pile back on the bus again. Yes, it counts, because they are technically 'walking'! With respect to some, I believe due to physical limitations this might be the only way to actually "walk" the Camino and I'm grateful they will get to feel the Camino Spirit.

I'm also grateful for the days when I rarely saw anyone.

So tomorrow we will begin early as usual. Wake up to my alarm at 4:50am, walk another 15 miles, and slowly inch our way to Santiago.

Day 28: Feels Like Day 128

Sarria to Portomarín
13.73 miles

As of today, we are less than 100km (62 miles) from Santiago. On Day 2, I was 790km (490 miles) from Santiago.

Every day for 28 days in a row, I've watched the sun come up. I feel strong. I spend my days fantasizing about walking into Santiago, but I'm also feeling heavy and weighed down with the realization of what I've done. Sometimes I don't believe it's me doing this.

The trail is still surprising me every single day.

Day 29: A Horrific Accident

Portomarin-Palas de Rei
16.7 miles
Off and on rain all day

Yesterday, there was a terrible accident at my albergue. A 77-year-old man fell down a flight of stairs. I was taking my afternoon siesta with my headphones in using my white noise app and I could hear his screams and the tumbling thuds all the way down. It makes my hands shake just to think of it. Yes, he was badly hurt; from what I could tell his arm was completely dislocated and twisted in addition to major contusions on his arms and head. There was a lot of blood.

He was traveling with his daughter and some friends. Thankfully he was not alone. Of course they were all hysterical. There were others in our albergue, none of whom spoke English, yet we could communicate quite effortlessly.

The most agonizing part was that it took 45 minutes for the ambulance to arrive. Can you imagine? He was conscious and talking after the fall so hopefully he will recover. But he is 77 years old.

It was his first and last day on the Camino.

I feel like these last few days I've been such a reluctant pilgrim. Every morning I get up with not one drop of excitement about walking. There have been 100 instances that could have been me falling down the stairs. So many days on the trail I was so tired and in such agony over blisters, or being sore, or hot, or cold, or alone with my thoughts. Most of these albergues are multiple stories, so we walk up flights of stairs with all of our gear after just walking for several hours. I shouldn't even call it walking because that implies what you do at an amusement park or the mall. It's not even hiking. It's not even really backpacking.

This is a pilgrimage across an entire country.

I've had a serious attitude about all the new pilgrims with their clean shoes and fresh faces. The fact is, I realize it's been a privilege for me to travel this path and remain (thus far) healthy. It's been a privilege to walk through hundreds of miles of villages, farms, hamlets, cities, towns and lonely mountains. Many times we have walked on private property and got a glimpse of life in rural Spain. I can't even count how many locals I've greeted with "hola" or a nod of my head while they go about their day-to-day business. It's extraordinary to be in the same spot where millions

Another day, another Knights Templar bridge to cross.

have traveled before. Saint Francis of Assisi walked on some of the same paths I have walked on. So did Suzy Orman. And Jenna Bush. And Angela Merkel. And Andrew McCarthy.

This journey has been harder than I've described. It has also been far more wonderful than I have described. But it cannot go on forever.

Three more days.

The symbols of the Knights Templar are all over this part of the Camino. They reassure me when I feel weak.

Day 30: 30th Bed of the Camino

Palas de Rei-Ribadisco da Baixo
16.4 miles

ARE YOU SERIOUS? I'VE BEEN DOING THIS FOR 30 DAYS!!!

The tread on my shoes...almost gone. The skin on my feet...totally shredded. My sock tan...epic.

Jules and I lollygagged our way over this trail today. It was almost as bad as yesterday when we stopped at least four times for snacks. Today we had our traditional two breakfasts and the most wonderful lunch of the entire Camino. Yes, I photographed it!

As I write this, I'm lying in my 30th bed of the Camino. Not counting the stopover in Lyon, France and the first night in SJPP, so I guess technically it's 32 beds. In this room there are 28 sets of bunk beds, almost all of them full. I don't remember what it's like to sleep in a room that isn't full of strangers.

Ducking in churches all day to avoid the rain.

Only two more days.

The trail is still magic even at this late stage.

Day 31: Day Before My Last Day

Ribadisco da Baixo-Pedrouzo
14.6 miles

We will walk into Santiago tomorrow.

The day before my last day on the Camino de Santiago.

Day 32: Santiago

Made it to Santiago.

Jules and I standing in front of the Santiago de Compostela Cathedral on the day we completed the 500-mile Camino de Santiago.

Post-Camino

Santiago, Spain
Day 1 Post-Camino

So, what next?

I'm just a girl from small town Chico, California with roots in Boring, Oregon who did this really cool thing. You can do this, too.

I wrote this to INSPIRE you.

My Camino family is one of the many reasons I made it through this experience. I love them dearly and after a month together we are closer than some relationships I've had over the course a lifetime. I know I will never forget them, and some I will be in contact with regularly.

Today I did the following:
- Woke up a little before 8am STARVING
- Got breakfast at a cafe with my friends
- Walked around Santiago a little
- Did laundry
- Sat around while laundry washed reading comments on my social media and tried not to cry at the outpouring of love
- Hung laundry out to dry
- FaceTimed with my bros, Marc & Scott

- Went out to lunch with friends and ate a ton of food
- Took a two-hour siesta
- Watched some pilgrims arrive to the square
- Walked around Santiago a little more then sat in a cafe and drank orange juice and got served an insane amount of free tapas
- Went on a Ferris wheel ride
- Ate the best churro I've ever had in my life
- Sat in the square listening to live music

Currently sitting in the kitchen of my albergue watching Jules do her nails. It was a good day. But also weird.

So, what's really next?

I am going to take a bus to Finisterre on Tuesday so I can visit the end of the world. Some of my friends will make the two-day walk, but I am finished walking.

I will return to Santiago on Thursday because Friday morning I fly to London to spend a week with friends.

Then I will go to Scotland for a week.

Then back to Pittsburgh.

Then back to Greensburg.

Then back to life.

But always carrying the magic of the Camino.

Alice's Daily Stages

Day	Date	Path	Mileage
1	6/21	SJPP to Roncesvalles	19
2	6/22	Roncesvalles to Zubri	14
3	6/23	Zubri to Pamplona	14
4	6/24	Pamplona to Puente La Renia	15.5
5	6/25	Puenta La Renia to Estella	14.5
6	6/26	Estella to Los Arcos	14.5
7	6/27	Los Acros to Logroño	18.2
8	6/28	Logroño to Nájera	18.5
9	6/29	Nájera to Santo Domingo	14
10	6/30	Santo Domingo to Belorado	14.85
11	7/1	Belorado to Atapuerca	20.3
12	7/2	Atapuerca to Burgos	13
13	7/3	Burgos to Hontanas	19.5
14	7/4	Hontanas to Boadilla	17.8

15	7/5	Boadilla to Carrion (car ride)	0
16	7/6	Carrion to Terradillos (halfway)	17
17	7/7	Terradillos to Calzadilla	14.6
18	7/8	Calzadilla to Mansilla	16.5
19	7/9	Mansilla to León	11.2
20	7/10	Rest day in León	0
21	7/11	León to Villadangos	13.6
22	7/12	Villadangos to Astorga	18.45
23	7/13	Astorga to Foncebadon	17.3
24	7/14	Foncebadon to Molinaseca	12.4
25	7/15	Molinaseca to Vega de Valcarce	19.6 (10.5 in car)
26	7/16	Vega de Valcarce to Fonfria	15
27	7/17	Fonfria to Sarria	20
28	7/18	Sarria to Portomarin	13.73
29	7/19	Portomarin to Palas de Rei	16.7
30	7/20	Palas de Rei to Ribadiso da Baixo	16.4
31	7/21	Ribadiso da Baixo to Pedrouzo	14.6
32	7/22	Pedrouzo to Santiago	12.6

Disclaimer: This may or may not be 100% accurate, but I tried to represent my stages with full integrity. In the end, I walked from SJPP to Santiago in 32 days.

Random Tips

- Notify your bank/cell phone carrier that you will be traveling abroad for an extended period of time.
- Take photos of your important documents (passport/medical cards/credit cards) and send them to your email.
- Look into getting an international calling/data plan with your cell phone carrier. For me it was worth it to have access to unlimited data. Comforting.
- Buy a European phone charger with ports for several cell phone cords so you don't hog up the electric wall socket all night.
- Write your name in black sharpie on EVERYTHING including your cell phone charger and cords. Make sure it's your name and not your initials.

If you have a smart phone:
- Turn location services on your phone so your friends/family can easily track your location.
- Take a selfie and/or photo every morning AND every night when you get to your albergue. It will stamp your photo with your location and time. It makes it easier to go back and figure out your mileage if you want an accurate tracking of your stages. It's just an easy way to track how far you walked every day.
- Download a white noise app and listen to it at night with your headphones in because the amount of noise made by 100 people sleeping in the same room is epic.

- Learn as much Spanish as possible/download apps on your phone to practice while you're spending hours on the trail.

Trust me:
- Take pictures all day, every day! THERE IS NO SUCH THING AS TAKING TOO MANY PICTURES!
- Take TONS of pictures of YOURSELF. Get people to take pics for you. Do it! Pictures with people are better than pictures without people.
- Wear more sunscreen than you've ever worn in your entire life
- Buy your shoes one size bigger than your regular size.

Buen Camino, Pilgrims.

Made in the USA
Middletown, DE
19 August 2020